Alina Degünther

Good and Evil in Shakespeare's King Lear and Macbeth

Anchor Compact

Degünther, Alina: Good and Evil in Shakespeare´s King Lear and Macbeth.
Hamburg, Anchor Academic Publishing 2013
Original title of the thesis: The Problems of Good and Evil in Shakespeare´s Tragedies
'King Lear' and 'Macbeth'

Buch-ISBN: 978-3-95489-064-4
PDF-eBook-ISBN: 978-3-95489-564-9
Druck/Herstellung: Anchor Academic Publishing, Hamburg, 2013
Additionally: Johannes Gutenberg-Universität Mainz, Mainz, Deutschland, Bachelorarbeit,
Mai 2012

Bibliografische Information der Deutschen Nationalbibliothek:
Die Deutsche Nationalbibliothek verzeichnet diese Publikation in der Deutschen
Nationalbibliografie; detaillierte bibliografische Daten sind im Internet über
http://dnb.d-nb.de abrufbar

Bibliographical Information of the German National Library:
The German National Library lists this publication in the German National Bibliography.
Detailed bibliographic data can be found at: http://dnb.d-nb.de

© Anchor Academic Publishing, ein Imprint der Diplomica® Verlag GmbH
http://www.diplom.de, Hamburg 2013
Printed in Germany

Table of Contents

1. Introduction

The concepts of good and evil, which can be understood and defined differently, are two broad and sapid concepts because of its diverse interpretations. The two abstract notions have been discussed throughout the centuries since the human existence and continue to be a dispute today. However, the meaning of good and evil was especially interesting in the middle Ages and Renaissance that will be introduced in the first part of this thesis. It will present the different origins of good and evil and examine how variously these concepts were perceived in the middle Ages and Renaissance. It should be pointed out that there was a great contrast in defining of good and evil in both centuries. While in the Middle Ages, good was supposed to come from God and evil from the Devil, in the Renaissance it was believed that good and evil originated from human beings. Moreover, these concepts were defined quite interestingly in early Renaissance. With existing hierarchical system and natural order in the universe in that age, good and evil were separated with the set of behavioural norms, so that evil was defined as opposite of good and meant every action which could cause the disruption of this order; a person performing an evil act was consequently called an evil person. However, in the late

Renaissance, which is also seen as the beginning of the modern era, the existing system of the universe has collapsed and the perception of good and evil has changed again. The concepts began to be distinguished as good, bad and evil acts. Moreover, they began to be problematic to be clearly defined, and the question also existed about struggle and victory of both forces. Additionally, the second part of the thesis will explore the problems of those concepts in terms of *King Lear* and *Macbeth*. It will deal with the problems of goodness of Cordelia and Banquo, evilness of Edmund and Lady Macbeth and badness of Lear and Macbeth. It will also identify how the characters turn to good, bad or evil side, whether they become creator or victims of evil, and finally reveal who of them can be called good, bad or evil person. Finally, the third part of the thesis will present the interpretation of the final scenes where both tragedies end with the coronation of the new king. It will explore the conflict of both forces and reveal what kind of force can actually win the struggle between good and evil in both plays. It will also deal with the problem of ambivalent depiction of the characters and examine the question of what is actually good and evil and how to define it in Shakespeare´s plays. So, the aim of the thesis is to explore the problems of the concepts of good and evil in terms of the tragedies *King Lear* and *Macbeth* and to identify to what extent the characters can be seen as good and evil. However, before exploring the characters it is worth introducing the varied meanings and definitions of the concepts of good and evil in Renaissance in order to be aware of how these concepts changed.

2. The Concepts of Good and Evil in Renaissance

First, it is important, curious and interesting comparing the vision of good and evil in the Middle Ages and Renaissance in order to understand how meanings of those concepts have changed from one century to another. In the middle Ages, it was believed that good initially originated from God and evil was created by the Devil. Medieval philosophers wondered about the origins of good and evil, and came to the conclusion that evil could not come from God. For example, Basel, theologian of the fourth century, claimed that "evil [was] neither uncreated nor created by God", while the pseudo-Dionysius, philosopher of the next century, stated that "evil [was] ...neither good nor productive of good..." (in Spivack, 17). Evil was seen as absence of good and God, and by that reason it was supposed to be originated from the Devil. Additionally, it was widely believed that human's soul was controlled by God and the Devil. For example, modern critic Davenport explains that wrongdoing of a man of that age was seen as "...corruption of human nature...by the Devil" (4). Moreover, in that age there was a tendency to personify the concepts of good and evil, and a good example of such personified notions of good and evil give the medieval morality plays. According to Davenport "…ideas of good and evil [were] represented by allegorical personification of human nature" (5), were good was presented in a figurative way, and was called virtue, which stand for all good qualities of a man. Evil was also personified and was called vice figure which stand for all negative qualities of a man. Supposing that supernatural beings can control a man´s soul, Virtue was thought to be messenger of God, whereas Vice was believed to be a messenger of the Demon. Moreover, the pattern of resolving conflict between good and evil was a simple one, because according to Davenport it was "[t]he pattern…of innocence, corruption and repentance" (5). So, it can be concluded that the traditional resolving of the conflict between good and evil was that goodness prevail evil, as a sinful man who had to repent and was saved by God.

While in the middle Ages it was believed that good and evil originated from God and the Devil, in the Renaissance the meaning of good and evil has changed. It was accepted that good and evil was a part of human nature and originally came from human beings. It should be pointed out that people of that age believed that the whole world was organized by God as a hierarchical system. Tillyard, researcher in the field of Elizabethan literature, states that people of that era believed in the existence of order in the universe, and adds that "order [was] the condition of all that follow[ed]" (11). Order was the condition of human existence and was present everywhere: in outer space, nature and society. People saw themselves as part of the hierarchical system and did not question the existence of the universe and order at all. Especially important for people was society, which was held by family and religious bonds. Modern critic Johnston explains that "faith, hope and charity [were] …responsibilities of that bonds which tie[d] together the family and the larger social groups", he adds that bonding gave individuals " a rich sense of social identity where each person's place in a hierarchical order [was] publicly acknowledged and honoured" (1). So, people did not question the existence of the universe, because they accepted a general order as a law. Moreover, they glorified God as a powerful organizer and feared the destruction of that system, which was the basis for their life. Relying on such social believes the distinction between good and evil was set by the norms of human behaviour. Evil was defined as opposite of good and was thought to be every action which could harm the natural order, especially society and family order, which was so important for people. Being deeply religious, people believed that denial of society or family bond was a sin, which could lead to a disruption of society order. Moreover, persons who were trying to harm the order by their wrongdoings were regarded as evil persons, because they could cause chaos, and disruption of natural order.

A good example of evil characters gives a Renaissance drama, where vice figure of morality plays developed in a villain person, who was seen as a cruel person involved in wrongdoing. Modern critic Coe explains that the audience of Elizabethan Age regarded villains as evil persons. He states that "[a]udience regarded them as types: black, illegitimate, deformed", he adds that the audience did not feel any sympathy for villains, because they were "unnaturally objective about their criminal nature" (69). In addition, one of such evil figures was Machiavel, the term derived from the Italian philosopher of the Renaissance Machiavelli who wrote the book *the Prince*, which was published in 1532, and in which he gave a special importance to the fact that a royal Prince according to circumstance should use his intelligence for manipulation of others in order to get and to maintain the power (cf. 22f). Such idea was regarded as an evil one, because deception and manipulation of others was seen as means directed against medieval society and was associated with disruption of society order. So, the theatrical performers acting in this way were also seen as despised and evil figures. Johnston explains, that in that age there was a banal vision of evil, because of existed social structure, he adds that there was a "frequent attempt to demonize such individuals, that is, to make them as abnormal and unnatural as possible" (1).

Moreover, while strong medieval beliefs in God and the Devil still continued to exist in the Renaissance, it was widely belied in the existence and power of witchcraft. It was supposed that witches were representatives of evil, because they could control a man´s soul and his fate. Contemporary researcher of literature Bailey comments on beliefs in witches of Renaissance age, saying that "…witches were accused of worshiping demons, renouncing their faith, and surrendering themselves completely to the service of the devil", he adds that belief in witchcraft fed to a large degree off common social structures" (4). So, the witches, whose supernatural practices were seen as a danger to natural order of society and religion, were thought to be in alliance with the Devil, because their power was directed against men.

In addition, being aware that consciousness of good and evil was incorporated in human nature, people believed in the Chain of Being, a concept which reflected human position in the hierarchy of the world. To apply the understanding of good and evil to human behaviour, people looked carefully at the position of man on the

Chain. According to Tillyard, the Chain started with God's throne at the top leading down to the lowest creatures, the beasts, where human had a central position on the great chain (cf.66). It was a simple position between good and evil, in which good was regarded as aspiration to be perfect, while evil was seen as a consequence of human sins. Humans believed that God gave man freedom of choice to move on the Chain in both directions. Twentieth century critic Spivack nicely describes the free choice of man on the Chain, saying: "Already part angel part beast, [man] can rise to more angelic stature to fulfil his spiritual aspiration, or he can degenerate to bestiality through surrender to animal nature" (24). Man was thought to be capable of two kinds of sins. As man had a soul as an angel, he could be overwhelmed with passions, which was called intellectual sin. Man had also physical desires as an animal, so he could be overwhelmed with physical satisfaction which was called physical sin. People believed that it depended on each person whether he followed his intellect or not in order to make a choice between good and evil.

However, in the late Renaissance the development of the individual takes place and, as the consequence of it, the hierarchical system of nature has collapsed. Now instead of glorifying God, art was directed to honour the individual. Church was not seen as a main centre of social activities, religion was not dominating anymore, and material world became a dominant part of life. Cultural historians of the nineteenth century Burckhardt enumerates many of those conditions which influenced the human consciousness: "Wealth and culture, so far as display and rivalry were not forbidden to them, a municipal freedom...a Church which... was not identical with the State - all these conditions undoubtedly favoured the growth of individual thought..." (71). All these factors also influenced the Renaissance vision of good and evil associated with God, order and disorder which began to disappear.

Moreover, new outlook on the world has sharply changed the spiritual and moral values in human consciousness. The principle of free human development becomes a main idea of the late Renaissance, and a religious sight at a person as on a sinful being who was thought to be evil has also been overcome. In this period, the new direction gets stronger which is called humanism. According to Oxford English Dictionary, under this word was understood a world outlook, proclaiming the supreme value of the human, confirming his rights of happiness and harmonious development (cf. 22). A person's earthly life and his struggle for happiness become the main idea of this epoch. In addition, new individuals of the Renaissance, who do not see natural order in the nature, have new opinion about good and evil. Johnston indicates that new individuals strongly oppose the medieval vision of morality and immorality, holding the opinion that man should apply his wit to shape his own future and to find his own sense of oneself without relying on what the community tells them what is right and wrong. They regard a good life as an assertion of their own individuality (cf. 1).

With new consciousness and outlook on the world, the great difference between good and evil began to disappear. Writers firstly argue the concepts of good and evil and make them problematic. For example, philosophers of the late seventeenth century Bacon and Montaigne discuss the concepts of good and evil and their degrees. Bacon raises the question what one can define as good and evil, saying: "In deliberatives the point is, what is good and what is evil, and of good what is greater, and of evil what is the less?" (149), then, he comments on the degree of their evaluation: "The reprehension of this colour is, that the good or evil which is removed, may be esteemed good or evil comparatively, and not positively or simply. So that if the privation of good, it follows not the former condition was evil, but less good" (156). Bacon makes a contrast with the medieval perception of those concepts, when evil

11

was seen as absence of good, and now he gives a new understanding of evil, pointing out that evil is not the absence of good, but is something what is less good. Besides, Montaigne disputes the concept of evil as common opinions or prejudice saying "that what we call evil is not evil in itself-or at least, whatever it is, that it depends on us to give it a different savour and a different complexion; for all it comes to the same thing" (33). Montaigne states that evil things can in fact be not evil at all, obviously referring to the fact the humans made things evil by the opinions they had which were shaped by the former hierarchical structures of the world and society.

So, the late Renaissance can be characterized as the beginning of the modern era, when attitude to human behaviour which could not be set by the norms of destroyed hierarchical order any more has changed. New perception of human individuality created the distinction between good, bad, and evil, and so the attitude to wrongdoers has also changed. What was morally wrong was not always seen as evil but as bad. Moreover, to define evil became problematic because of its ambiguous nature. According to the critic of Renaissance morality Heller: "Evil [was seen as] a great force, sinful, amoral. But at the same time [was] definitely not an absolutely negative force" (313). So, the next chapter will clarify to what extent the characters in Shakespeare´s plays *King Lear* and *Macbeth* can be seen as good and evil from the new perspective and explore the problems of good and evil. First, the goodness of Cordelia and Banquo will be presented and clarified in the following pages.

3. Good and Evil in *King Lear* and *Macbeth*

3.1 Forces of Goodness: Cordelia and Banquo

Cordelia represents a symbol of idealized goodness because of her manifestation of the absolute and pure love for her father, Lear. She reveals her true feelings in the love test, in which Lear trials the emotions of his three daughters in order to divide his Kingdom among them. It is sufficiently to note that Cordelia, Lear's youngest daughter, did not deceive her father, whereas her sisters did. Needless to say, she felt that her father should know of her obvious affections without the need for frivolous words. Cordelia acts against the test, because she tries to aware her father in the false-ness of her sisters' love to him, as she knows that their love is not as pure as they profess. Her meek sentences reveal her act against Goneril's flattering: "What shall Cordelia speak? Love, and be silent" (1.1.62). She continues her speech against Regan's fraud: "Then poor Cordelia, /And yet not so, since I am sure my love's/ More ponderous than my tongue" (1.1.76-78). Cordelia tries to warn her father that he is being deceived by the flattering of her wicked sisters. In addition, Cordelia's way of speaking demon-strates her true and chaste love for Lear. She does not even make an attempt to convey her feelings by words when she speaks: "Unhappy that I am, I cannot heave [m]y heart into my mouth (1.1.91). Cordelia is not able to flatter the way her wicked sisters do and her virtuous love apparently makes her mute. She is so truthful and charitable, that she cannot express her love through words, because seemingly the words cannot describe her feeling. Hence, her faithful love appears to be more than words and cannot be expressed through an eloquent speech.

Moreover, Cordelia´s great love reveals her temperament of a sincere daughter who shows fidelity to her father. Cordelia is neither proud nor stubborn when she speaks to her father: "I love you majesty /According to my bond, no more no less" (1.1.92-3). Her sentence exposes that Cordelia is different from her bad sisters because she shows her honesty and generosity, and truly describes her feeling remaining truthful to her bond. Moreover, her emphasis of the word bond indicates that Cordelia acknowledges the bonding between parents and children. She is a character who supports the medieval view of the society based on interrelation of bonds and who acknowledges moral order in the nature. So, her love is also traditional and manifests the daughter´s chaste nature.

Cordelia is a pure goodness and remains so until her tragic end. She does not show any change in her disposition throughout the play, and that makes her different from other characters that will be presented in the next chapters. Cordelia was silent during the love test because she quietly answered to her father when he asked about her feelings: "Nothing my lord" (1.1.87), and she continued to be quiet in the reconciliation scene, when she met her father again (4.7.40f). After being unjustly banished by her own father during the love test because of her short answers, which Lear did not accepted, Cordelia appears again in the scene where she is being forgiven by her father and can finally restore friendly relationship with him. When Lear is asking for her forgiveness, she answers: "Alack, alack (4.7.40). And so I am, I am (4.7.70). No cause, no cause "(4.7.75). Again, she remains emotionless as at the beginning, and it seems that she does not have any compassion to herself but only to her father. That gives an impression that Cordelia is very unselfish and remains true to her filial love despite of her unfair treatment. Moreover, Cordelia, whose love is immense for her father, shows her willingness to suffer for him, what becomes obvious during her imprisonment with Lear. Being in capture with Lear, Cordelia shows her tears to him (cf.4.7.71) and her weeping seemingly reveals her pity and compassion not for herself but for her father. So she is aware of her father's suffering and knows that he endures pain because he treated her inequitable and was blinded by her wicked sisters' flattering. So, Cordelia wants to act in any way to relieve his pain, what can be achieved only on the cast of her own life. Only when Cordelia loses her life, and Lear sees her beloved daughter dead, he is seemingly relieved from suffering and dies not in despair but as Foakes notes in joy (cf. 139).

Cordelia's goodness which is apparently spiritual and self-sacrificial merits an admiration for its high purity. Cordelia even resembles a Christ the way she suffers because she is ready to sacrifice her life for her father. Modern critic Anderson nicely comments on Cordelia´s sacrificing nature: "[Cordelia] made an investment in the good of another - an investment that is necessarily self-sacrificial…" (280); she gives her life in the sake of her father´s good. So, there is no doubt in Cordelia´s virtuous and conciliatory nature of goodness and her moral purity. So, the problem is not in her good nature, but in her death.

Cordelia´s perfect goodness is apparently tragic which contributes to the conflict between good and evil. On the first sight, her death is morally unintelligible because it is difficult to conceive why such a perfect and innocent character should die. Cordelia has reconciled with her father and has been forgiven by him, so that there seems to be no need for her farther punishment. Her death appears to be unbearable not only for the audience, but for the good characters such as Kent and Edgar as well, which is obvious in their reactions to her death: "It this the promis'd end? Or image of that horror" (5.3.264-5). Both of them express their sad emotions when Lear carries the body of dead Cordelia in his arms. So, she cannot be justified or blamed for her actions because her ending appears to be simply pitiful and tragic. However, her death can be understood as a loss of a battle between good and evil. Cordelia's goodness is ready to struggle with her bad sisters who saw their father as merely a powerful object. Nevertheless, with all her efforts to fight she remains defenseless: she fails against evil forces and loses her life because she is too perfect to struggle with evil, and hence she can be regarded as a greatest victim in *King Lear*. In this respect, Cordelia is an ideal goodness, who perishes in the world which is full of outrage. Her dead body resembles a Christ, but as Anderson states a Christ who is not crucified but rather resurrected (cf. 262). It is seemingly true that with all her perfection, evil forces have destroyed her goodness, and in the struggle between good and evil she loses her life. This happened because Cordelia's vision of evil is too naive, and she is seemingly too innocent thinking that she could win the battle between good and evil. Her perfect nature obviously does not fit to the outside world full of violence. In this respect, *King Lear* can support the statement that goodness can be easily destructed by human evil, despite of the strongest efforts to struggle against it. Example of Cordelia´s fate also implies that moral goodness may also have evil consequences.

Another interesting character presented in *Macbeth* is Banquo, who on the first sight embraces all characteristics of goodness, but who, in contrast to Cordelia, changes his pure morality and becomes corrupted by evil temptation as the play progresses. At the beginning of the play, Banquo and his closest friend Macbeth are being tempted by the witches who in Shakespeare´s time were seen as demonic powers willing to foretell future. The witches addressing Macbeth prophesied him the future position of the Thane of Cawdor and later the throne of the King of Scotland (1.1.46f). While the weird sisters were addressing Macbeth, Banquo revealed his mistrust to them, saying:

What are these,
So wither'd and so wild in their attire,
That look not like th' inhabitants o' th' earth

Are ye fantastical, or that indeed
Which outwardly ye show? (1.3.38-54)

At this point, Banquo recognizes them as inhuman beings, and even wonders if they are real. Farther, being curious Banquo asks the witches to foretell him the future, saying: "Speak then to me, who neither beg, nor fear/ Your favours nor your hate" (1.3.57-61). Despite of his curiosity, and discovering from the witches that he will get the line of kings (cf.1.3.67), Banquo reveals in his speech that he does not fear neither the witches nor their hate, because he seemingly thinks that they are not able to control or to influence the future as long as they can only foretell it. In contrast to Macbeth, who became inquisitive about the prophecy, Banquo remains mistrustful to them, and hence shows his moral goodness by avoiding evil temptation. Even when prophesy about Thane of Cawdor became true for Macbeth, Banquo remained doubtful to the witches considering them as demonic powers saying: "What! Can the Devil speak true?" (1.3.107). So despite of the truthfulness of the witches prophecies, Banquo remains unimpressed by them without showing any further interest to know more about their speeches. In this way, Banquo unveils his clear distinction between goodness and evilness enticement and trusts himself not to be tempted by the evil. Moreover, Banquo who is able to distinguish between the honesty and witches truth-telling warns Macbeth, who in opposite to Banquo, is blinded by the witches' predictions concerning his future fate. Banquo cautions Macbeth that the weird sisters may deceive him saying:

And oftentimes, to win us to our harm,
The instruments of Darkness tell us truths;
With us with honest trifles, to betray's
In deepest consequence (1.3.122-26)

Banquo suggests that the witches' prophecies are powerless as long as people do not trust their speeches, and they are not able to inflict harm they may wish. Here Banquo refers to the prophecy predicting Macbeth the throne, which, on opinion of Macbeth, can be fulfilled only on the cast of Duncan´s murder, the present King of Scotland.

However, in the next scene, Banquo's goodness becomes dubious because of his denial to expose the truthful prophecies to the present king. While Banquo together with Duncan were approaching Macbeth's castle, Banquo seemed to be free from the thoughts about the witches what is evident in his speech:

This guest of summer,
The temple-haunting martlet, does approve,
By his loved mansionry, that the heaven's breath
Smells wooingly here: no jutty, frieze,
Buttress, nor coign of vantage, but this bird
Hath made his pendent bed, and procreant cradle:
Where they most breed and haunt, I have observ'd
The air is delicate (1.6.3-10).

Here, Banquo nicely describes the beauty of the nature which is surely associated with the sense of peace and natural order. Such pleasing description also represents goodness and morality that Banquo had at the beginning of the play, when he warned Macbeth not to trust the witches. However, at this point Banquo fails to tell Duncan about the witches' prophecies and his goodness becomes doubtful. While he is aware of the witches' true speeches, he denies to caution Duncan about their prophecies and possible danger for him, and hence to do good for him. Later that night, during which the murder of Duncan will take place, Banquo is oppressed by the weird thoughts that he reveals in his soliloquy:

A heavy summons lies like lead upon me,
And yet I would not sleep: merciful powers,
Restrain in me the cursed thoughts that nature
Gives way to in repose! (2.1.6-9)

Now Banquo is seemingly disturbed by the thoughts of the moral guilt that he endures because of his concealing of the evil prophecies from Duncan. His fear to sleep suggests the distortion of his mind, and his possible efforts to pray reveal his attempt to keep his right reason under control. However, despite of his prayer, Banquo avoids doing goodness for Duncan because he apparently hopes that the prophecies will come true and he, on the cast of Macbeth's crime, will become a father of many kings (cf. 3.1.5). For that reason, his goodness so nicely presented at the beginning starts to descent into evil.

Finally, Banquo has apparently forgotten his warning not to trust the witches so that his ambition and the prophecies perverted his mind. After Duncan has been murdered by Macbeth, Banquo gives an impression of a brave and honest man, who states that he will stand "in the great hand of God" and fight against every "treasonous malice"(2.3.128f). At this point, Banquo´s speech reminds us of his previous prayer for his moral stability. However, he quickly breaks his promising statement by the fact that he will never reveal Macbeth as Duncan´s murderer. Banquo, knowing alone about the witches and being suspicious about their prophecies, never exposes them to anyone until the last day of his life. His ambitious mind is obviously yielded to evil and, despite of his mistrust to the witches,

Banquo begins to believe in them. In his final soliloquy, he confesses that he is sure about the truthfulness of the prophecies and hopes to get the line of kings:

Thou has it now: King, Cawdor, Clamis, all
As the Weird Women promised; and I fear,2424

If there come truth from them,
(As upon thee, Macbeth, their speeches, shine),

May they not be my oracles as well,
And set me up in hope? (3.1.1-10)

Lastly, Banquo's hope to get the royal power never comes in fulfillment because he, on the order of Macbeth, has been brutally killed by murderers (cf.3.3.18). However, Banquo dies not as an innocent victim and a good man as he gave an impression at the beginning of the play, but as a man corrupted by evil. As Bradley points out: "[the killed Banquo was] not the innocent soldier who met the Witches and daffed their prophecies aside, nor the man who prayed to be delivered from the temptation of his dreams" (386). So, in contrast to Cordelia, Banquo manifested the question-ability of his goodness expressed in his denial to resist evil entice-ment. It also implies that the power of good can change its direc-tion toward bad. Furthermore, the following chapter will also demonstrate the ambiguity of the evil nature of the characters such as Edmund and Lady Macbeth, who in opposite to the forces of goodness represent the forces of evil.

3.2. Forces of Evil: Edmund and Lady Macbeth

Edmund who, on the first sight, seems to embrace many traits of an evil person for the sake of power is a great villain in *King Lear*. The enticement to call him evil person is big, because he undoubtedly can be compared to Machiavellian Prince who had an evil reputation in Renaissance era. Edmund reveals his Machiavellian qualities by the way he manipulates virtue and truth for his own profit. He shows his greedy, self-interested desire to attain power by deceiving his father, Gloucester, and brother, Edgar. It should be said that Edmund, illegitimate son of Earl of Gloucester, knows that his legitimate son Edgar, will succeed all father´s properties, and being jealous of him, uses his intellect in order to get the throne. He manipulated his father's good nature by showing him Edgar´s false letter directed against Gloucester (cf.1.2.55-60). He also cheated Edgar saying that his father is against him and persuading him to flee from kingdom (cf.1.2.170-5). He betrayed Gloucester and Edgar, seeing them as mere objects for manipulation:

A credulous father and a brother noble,
Whose nature is so far from doing harms
That he suspects none- on whose foolish honesty
My practices ride easy (1.2.176-180).

So, Edmund successfully uses his intellect in order to get the crown. So, there is no doubt that Edmund is the Machiavellian character in *King Lear* for the reasons discussed above.

However, the temptation to call Edmund evil may be misleading, because the Machiavellian tactics he uses can be seen as not evil at all. It is true that Machiavelli was a disdained evil figure in his age; but Machiavellian tactic is not evil as Renaissance thinkers assumed. Modern critics explain that to be Machiavellian does not mean to be evil. For example, Tung emphasizes that "A Machiavellian hero is simply a successful hero, a hero who can win power and hold it" (74). Roe has the same opinion indicating that "Machiavelli at no point advocates the practise of evil as acceptable in itself despite what his many detractors then and now have said; he concedes rather that evil sometimes has to be used" (15). So, the Machiavellian Prince who wants to maintain power has to be prepared not to be virtuous and use tricky tactic according to circumstances. Edmund is successful to a large extent as he uses this tactic with a high intelligence, and it works to get what he desires. So, on the one hand, it seems to be true that Edmund is selfish, cruel, deceitful and wise. On the other hand, he practically achieved a high position with these qualities, like Machiavelli's Prince with all these qualities would.

Moreover, villainous Edmund also has some positive qualities in his personality. He shows some good nature by trying to justify his Machiavellian traits which were motivated by some reasons. He was born as an illegitimate son of Gloucester, and his elder brother Edgar had acquired all heritages. He is humiliated by his own father for his bastardy. In Edmund's presence, Gloucester openly speaks with Kent about his bastardy and asserts that his illegitimacy embarrasses him: "His breeding, sir, hath been at my charge. I have so often blushed to acknowledge him that now I am brazed to´ it (1.1.8-10), he continues saying that "the whoreson must be acknowledged" (1.1.22-3). As a consequence, Edmund expresses his anguish in his first soliloquy:

Thou, Nature, art my goddess; to thy law
My services are bound. Wherefore should I
Stand in the plague of custom, and permit
The curiosity of nations to deprive me?
For that I am some twelve or fourteen moon-shines
Lag of a brother? Why bastard? Wherefore base?
Now, gods, stand up for bastards (1.2.1-22).

His speech reveals that Edmund blames the nature for his illegitimacy and sees no fault in his bastardy. Thus, he sees his bastardy as justification for his villainy and his bastard feature becomes the starting point for his wicked actions. As considered a bastard, he decides to act as a bastard, the way as Machiavelli acts, manipulating his father and brother for his own sake.

Moreover, it should be said that Edmund´s driving force is not a passion for revenge, but is a self-interest, greed and egoism. Edmund does not seeking revenge, because he does not hate his father and brother. He has no reason for hatred which is expressed in Gloucester´s words: "But I Have a son, sir, by order of law, some year elder than this, who yet is no dearer in my account" (1.1.19-20). Gloucester seems to love his both sons equally, but his statement "by order of law" suggests that only Edgar will get the heir. Edmund is simply jealous toward Edgar, who by law succeeds all father´s property. So, he has no certain wish to hurt his brother or father. It again confirms the fact that Edmund thinks rationally simply regarding Gloucester and Edgar as his nuisance to become an Earl.

Moreover, Edmund acts individually denying the traditional society view of the early Renaissance which implicates that society is held by family bonds. In his dialog with Edgar he talks about inequality between parents and children and how the ties of social bonds break: "…the unnaturalness between the child and the parent…banishment of friends… dissipation of cohorts, nuptial breaches…" (1.2.144-7). His speech implies his understanding of the importance of human actions and individuality. Thus, he decides to act individually by denying traditional bonding, respect and virtue for his father and brother. It seems that there is no standard virtue for him, which determines the values of good person. He only wants to get a better position in life, which means for him prestige and power. Edmund can be characterized as a new individual of Renaissance, who does not acknowledge a natural order in society.

Moreover, Edmund shows his positive trait by trying to repent in order to justify his immoral actions. It should be pointed out that Edmund, who also desired to get the power of Lear's Kingdom, in the battle against Lear's forces captured him and Cordelia and gave an order to execute them (cf.5.3.29-35). However, Edmund decides to do some good before his death by revealing his order to kill Lear and Cordelia, saying:

I pant for life. Some good I mean to do,
Despite of mine own nature. Quickly send-

Be brief in it- to the castle, for my writ
Is on the life of Lear and on Cordelia;
Nay, send in time (5.3.240-245).

He seems to feel compassion for his father, who by the word of
Edgar died "passion and grief" (5.3.197) because of knowing the
truth about Edmund's deception Although some critics such as
Lökse and Coe are convinced that Edmund cannot repent augment-
ing it by the fact that he is unfeeling and cold villain (cf. Lökse
1960, 114; cf. Coe 1972, 60). Edmund is not cold at all even if he
gives such an impression. He tries to repent because he seemingly
feels pity for his dead father.

So, Edmund is not an evil person; evil is too strong word for him.
Edmund has no intention to kill somebody and he even reveals his
order to kill Lear and Cordelia. Edmund just acts immorally
throughout the play because he neglects traditional bonding,
respect and virtue for his family for his own advantage. On the
other hand, he also shows some positive traits by trying to justify
his actions through his soliloquy and repentance. So, Edmund can
be characterized as bad son and wicked person in *King Lear*.
Moreover, his Machiavellian tactics that he used successfully and
that is morally wrong implies that immoral actions can also have a
good result.

Another problematic villain presented in Shakespeare is Lady Macbeth, whose villainous nature is motivated not by greed but by passion. The first impression the audience gets of her is as of self-interested, ruthless and heartless woman. Her self-interest is expressed in her strong desire to achieve the crown of Scotland on the cast of Duncan´s murder. Being informed form Macbeth´s letter, that he will become a king according to the witches' prophecies, she immediately becomes confident that her husband will get the crown, and associates the witches' prophecies with murder of Duncan. However, Lady Macbeth is aware that he husband is not masculine enough to perform a cruel deed, saying: "Yet do I fear thy nature/ It is too full o´th´milk of/ human kindness" (1.5.15-16), and that makes her upset. However, within a few minutes after her speech, she has been informed by the messenger that Duncan will come to their castle that night (cf. 1.5.31). From this moment she immediately seems to become be overwhelmed by the passion to kill the King by herself and she reveals her cruel intentions in her monologue:

Come, you spirits
That tend on mortal thoughts, unsex me here,
And fill me, from the crown to the toe, top full

Of direst cruelty! Make thick my blood,
Stop up th´ access and passage to remorse (1.5.40-44).

However, it seems that she cannot be an evil person because she is too strongly overwhelmed with passion. Yet Lady Macbeth is not aware of the evil consequences of murder that she plans thoroughly, and her speech is full of passion, as if her mind and soul were overwhelmed by evil temptation for an hour before the murder. She asks the help of evil ghosts to "unsex" her, in order to get rid of her female qualities, associated with pity and compassion. Critic Knight emphasizes her strong will and ambition, saying: "The scope and sweep of her evil passion is tremendous, irresistible, and ultimate. She is an embodiment- for one mighty hour- of evil [which is] absolute and extreme" (152). So, Lady Macbeth cannot be an evil person because she only shows the weakness of her soul obsessed with evil passion for some time. In addition, she is not a cruel person in her nature because she; despite of her strong efforts to be disposed of her woman qualities, cannot murder Duncan by herself, and she finally ambitiously encourages Macbeth to commit murder saying: "… you shall put/ This night´s great business into my dispatch…" (1.5.67-8). Here Lady Macbeth reveals her wish to play only the second role in the murder of Duncan, what is seemingly her efforts to persuade Macbeth to do it, and her inability to commit murder by herself shows her true womanhood.

Moreover, Lady Macbeth remains a natural woman, what is expressed in her gradual downfall after the murder of Duncan committed by Macbeth. She thought that the cruel deed would not make her tough, but now she cannot elude the emotional consequences of what she has promoted her husband to do. She seems to be naive when she tells her husband that "A little water will clear us of this deed" (2.2.66-67), because in reality she cannot withstand her guilty consciousness. As a consequence she loses her emotional composure, becomes weak and falls apart. This begins with her fainting after the news about Duncan´s murder becomes overt for all (cf.2.3.117-123). Moreover, she cannot bear her guilty thoughts about killed Duncan throughout the play, and she becomes gradually mad. So, Lady Macbeth slipped up thinking that she could suppress any feeling of humanity in herself and become an insensible woman, but it appeared impossible for her to separate herself from her own woman nature.

Lady Macbeth´s sleepwalking scene is the most visible sign of her misery and madness. Suffering from her guilty memories, Lady Macbeth consequently falls apart, and walks in the castle at night during her sleep. This becomes obvious from the speech of a gentlewoman and doctor, who came in order to investigate her illness:

Doct. How came she by that light?
Gent. Why, it stood by her: she has light by her continually; 'tis her command
Doct. You see, her eyes are open.
Gent. Ay, but their sense are shut.
Doct. What is it she does now? Look, how she rubs her hands.
Gent. It is an accustom'd action with her, to seem thus washing her hands. I have known her continue in this a quarter of an hour. (5.20.29)

The final scene of Lady Macbeth's illness indicates that even in her dreams she is incapable to find peace in her mind because of her culpable consciousness. Her soul is apparently tormented by guilty memories about her ambitious intentions to push Macbeth toward murder, so that now she constantly tries to wash her hands, and what seemingly symbolizes her wish to clean herself from her guilt which disturbs her even in her sleep. Lady Macbeth obviously became mad because she imagines bloody spots on her hands, which she cannot get rid of, and which symbolize blood of innocent Duncan who was killed unjustly. Her screams (cf. 5.1.33-5) indicate her inner conflict, the great misery, and the struggle between good and evil inside herself. The light which she always

34

has with her reveals that she tries to protect herself from her madness and her fear of darkness means that she cannot withstand her guilty memories. Her repetition and emphasis of the word "bed" (cf. 5.1. 63-5) indicates that she is looking for a long and quiet sleep needed for good and innocent people. Her guilty consciousness makes her mad and weak, and as long as she cannot bear it anymore, she commits suicide.

So, Shakespeare's villains such as Edmund and Lady Macbeth do not appear to be evil persons at all. While Edmund neglects the traditional bonding and shows individualistic traits in order to achieve the final goal, Lady Macbeth is obsessed with strong passion. Other tragic characters such as Lear and Macbeth whose good and evil nature seems to be more interesting and complicated will be presented in the next chapter.

3.3. Challenging Concepts of Good and Evil: Lear and Macbeth

In the opening scene, Lear appears to be an absolute and strong king that manifests his goodness. Lear is a dominant person in his country who has ruled his kingdom for a long period of time. Johnston calls Lear a "king of his country and a patriarch of his family", he adds that "everyone looks at him as the source of order and meaning in the society" (1). Lear is proud of being a king and remains so during the love-test, which he organized to test the feelings of his three daughters towards him in order to divide his kingdom among them. However, during the love-test scene, Lear appears to be "at the heart of evil in the play" (Beauregard 2008, 204), because he, being deceived by his wicked daughters, made an error which caused the tragedy of his whole life. To his question "Which of you shall we say doth love us most" (1.1.51), Regan and Goneril answered with flattery, whereas his beloved daughter Cordelia answered with sincerity, saying: "I love you majesty according to my bond" (1.1.92). Lear, believing in flattery, banish-es Cordelia from his kingdom because he supposes that she humiliated his royal dignity openly. At this point, it becomes obvious that Lear, who is being deluded by his wicked daughters, is not an evil person. The evil comes from ungrateful Regan and Goneril, and their evil is seemingly the lack of respect to their father because of their self-interested desire for power. By their flattering, Lear is obviously led into error by mistreating his beloved daughter Cordelia and banishes her from his kingdom with the words:

Here I disclaim all my paternal care,
Propinquity and property of blood,
And as a stranger to my heart and me,
Hold thee from this forever. (1.1.114-7)

At this point, Lear shows his pride and reveals his angry reaction to Cordelia by rejecting her. He is apparently an ambitious person who is dominated by his emotions and is unable to control them, and he expresses his rage by banishing Cordelia because he cannot accept her treatment of him. He is unable to accept anything which does not adjust to his will, and that what injures his own identity. Moreover, the love-test alone manifests Lear´s individualistic traits. His attempt to trial the daughters' feelings reveals that Lear cannot separate the duties of the king and that of the father and tells the reader that Lear has a narrow understanding of how the society is held together. The act of banishing Cordelia implies that Lear´s strong sense of identity allows him to break the natural bond based on family relations between himself and Cordelia. For Lear authority appears to be more important than the family bond, as he does not worry about the injustice made to Cordelia. He obviously accepts only those who act according to his will and misunderstands people like Cordelia, who acted against his wishes. So, Lear acts individually according to the new views of Renaissance, in which family relations are less important than one´s own prestige. Moreover, his individualistic view of the world allows Lear to misjudge the morality of the good daughter and that of the wicked daughters, so that he misunderstands the good intentions of Cordelia´s speech and becomes blinded by the foul intentions of Goneril and Regan´s flattering.

However, in the next scene, Lear begins to face the consequences of the love-test. After dividing his Kingdom and retiring, Lear seeks shelter by Goneril, who again revealing her wicked nature, turned against Lear. Now, Lear is unable to recognize neither himself nor his daughter anymore and begins to lose his mind asking other people about his identity, saying: "Does any here know me? Why, this is not Lear... Who is it that can tell me who I am?" (1.4. 216-221). Here Lear feels helplessness to the hostile behaviour of Goneril, and falling into anguish, he proclaims: "Life and death. I am ashamed … Old fond eyes,/ Beweep this cause again, I´ll pluck ye out" (1.4.290). Lear´s wish to pluck out his eyes suggests that he begins to lose his mind because of his shame to recognize the wickedness of his daughter, whom he trusted. Thereafter, Lear seeks Regan trying to find shelter, respect and care from her. However, Lear finds out that Regan acts the same way as her sister Goneril did. Both daughters tell Lear that he does not have any further need in their care because he will be treated by their servants (cf.2.2.430-5). Here Lear undergoes a further change in his mind, which is obvious in his soliloquy:

You heavens, give me that patience, patience I need!
You see me here, you gods, a poor old man,
As full of grief as age, wretched in both!
If it be you that stirs these daughters' hearts
Against their father (2.2.461-4)

Lear seems to be unable to control his thoughts and his mind weakens further. So, he turns to the gods in hope that he will receive patience to his soul and his mind from them. He imagines that the gods, being unfair to him, cause him suffering. However, the injustice inflicted to Lear comes not from the gods or heaven, but from human evil, which originates from "the hardness of human heart" when it is driven by "passion and malice" (Beauregard 2008, 218). It is Lear's ambition and pride which led him to his mental blindness and his daughter's unkindness drove him into madness.

Moreover, Lear's suffering inflicted by his wicked daughters continues throughout the play but is mostly expressed in the storm scene. Thinking about his unkind daughters, Lear becomes unable to repress the feeling of being disgraced and recognizes his suffering while being on the heath. Here Lear reveals his rage and struggles against Nature, saying: "And thou, all-shaking thunder/ Strike flat the thick rotundity o′ th′ world (3.2.6-9). Now he is ready to believe that he became a victim of Nature because he acknowledges his downfall from being a king to being a mere beggar. So he pities himself with the words: "Here I stand your slave/ A poor, infirm, weak and despised old man… I am a man/ More sinned against than sinning" (3.2.19f, 59f). Here Lear perceives the force of his wrong action and acknowledges that he gave his power to his ungrateful daughters who in reality act against him. Moreover, during the storm, Lear considers Nature as his enemy, calling the rain as the "pitiless storm" (3.4.29) and he realizes the force of unjust human suffering, when he says: "Expose thyself to feel what wretches feel" (3.4.33-4). Here Lear pities himself, because he identifies himself with poor people and understands how it is to be poor and to be treated unjustly.

In addition, Lear′s highest peak of madness, but also his breakthrough to understand humanity and moral values are introduced when he meets Edgar during the storm, disguised as poor Tom, who has also been unjustly treated by his brother Edmund. Lear feels compassion for him because he regards a naked beggar as a sufferer of the storm, as he is. So, Lear tears off his clothes to identify himself with Poor Tom, saying:

Unaccommodatcd man is no more but such a poor,
bare, forked animal as thou art. Off, off, you lendings!
come, unbutton here. (3.4.105-7)

Lear´s inability to deal with reality to accept himself as a human and to realize the wickedness of his daughters drives him into madness and consequently into identification with Poor Tom. However, through his madness, Lear learns to deal with reality and finds a new view of the world. He recognizes the helplessness of Poor Tom, and through his compassion he learns to be human. Only through his downfall from a powerful king to a poor beggar, Lear becomes a new man, who from his pride, ambition and self-pity learns to understand human moral values based on love, compassion and family relations. In addition, through his fall, Lear learns to understand to be human and to distinguish between good and evil: that is sincerity of Cordelia and flattery of his wicked daughters by whom he has been deceived for a long time.

So, in the fourth Act, Lear´s recovery from madness is expressed in his recognition of Cordelia. Lear, after a long sleep caused by his madness, returns to reality and recognizes his chaste daughter, saying: "Do not laugh at me;/ For, as I am a man, I think this lady/ To be my child Cordelia (4.7.68-70). He also recognizes himself as her father and is ready to reconcile with her. Lear recognizing himself as a "foolish fond old man" (4.7.60), comes out of his madness and finds himself from being an absolute king to a human being. He recognizes the injustice towards Cordelia and shows his humanity in revealing his paternal love to her. Furthermore, being in capture with Cordelia by the order of Edmund, Lear asks for her mercy (5.3.11). At this point, Lear "reached purification" (Lökse 1960, 158), and it seems that he repents his pride, and his foolish-ness expressed in his unwillingness to get his throne back. Instead, he wishes to stay in prison, where he can enjoy the life with Cordelia, saying: "Come, let´s away to prison: We two alone will sing like birds i´ the cage" (5.3.8-9). Now it seems that Lear has perceived that the family bond is more important than his authority and prestige.

Unfortunately, Lear has to face the consequences of human evil until his tragic death. Lear´s suffering continues before he dies and he cannot bear the result of human evil- that is the unjust death of Cordelia, who has been hanged by the order of Edmund. Again, Lear, for whom the life seems senseless without Cordelia, becomes aware of unjust human suffering. He, asking the question: "Why should a dog, a horse, a rat have life/ And thou no breath at all?" (5.3.305-6) has no answer to it. Trying to convince himself that Cordelia is still alive, Lear is unable to deal with the consequences of human evil, and for that reason regrettably dies.

Another victim of evil is the successful warrior, Macbeth, who is also characterized as a good man at the beginning of the play. He is a fighter, who successfully defended his country, and a "highly esteem member of a social group", who interacts with nobles and is a very faithful toward his king Duncan (Johnston 1999, 1). Macbeth has a precious wife and owns a castle. He too, as Lear, becomes a victim of evil; however, he becomes a sufferer of his own ambition because he, never being deceived by human evil, alone decides to act that way, which consequently destroyed him.

The tragedy of his life begins with the prophecies of the three witches, whom Macbeth met when he was returning from the battle against Ireland. The supernatural beings address him with the words:

1Witch. All hail, Macbeth! hail to thee, Thane of Claims!
2Witch. All hail, Macbeth! hail to thee, Thane of Cawdor!
3Witch.All hail, Macbeth! that shalt be king hereafter. (1.3.47-50)

At first Macbeth denies the possibility to become The Thane of Cawdor, and so he tries not to be tempted by the witches. However, after the second prophecy became true, he immediately changes his mind and about the killing of Duncan: "This supernatural soliciting/ Cannot be ill; cannot be good" (1.3.130-1). Here Macbeth describes the deed as partly good and partly evil. On the one hand, the murder cannot be evil, because Macbeth will get the crown, so it is good. On the other hand, the murder is morally wrong, so it means that it cannot be good. Here Macbeth seems to fall into confusion to define what is morally good or wrong, and it seems that he begins to fear his thought of killing for the crown. He even assumes that he will become a king without murdering, saying: "If chance will have me King, why,/ Chance my crown me,/ Without my stir "(1.3.144-5). His possible decision to deny murder gives an impression that the good side of Macbeth´s consciousness will win over the evil one. However, the evil side of Macbeth is still in action, so that he cannot leave so easily the thought from his mind that he can become a king. Again, he thinks about the "black and deep desires" and imagines the murder (1.4.51), which he actually fears to do. So, it seems that Macbeth´s consciousness is divided into two parts: the first part of him is delighted with the vision of himself as a king, and the second part of him cannot approve the immorality of action and its consequences. Macbeth also knows that he will have to pay a great cost for the evil deed, which he is thinking about. In his soliloquy he expresses his fear of punishment:

But in this cases,
We still have judgment here; that we but teach
Bloody instructions, which, being taught, return
To plague th´inventor : this even- handed Justice
Commends th´ingredience of our poison´d chalice
To our own lips. (1.7.7-12)

In his consciousness Macbeth fears the justice and the punishment of being murdered. He is apparently afraid that someone, who morally resembles him, will kill him for the same purpose. Nevertheless, the imagination of being a king obsesses him, and he cannot stop thinking about the murder of Duncan. Macbeth himself refers to his desire as ambition, saying: "I have no spur/ To prick the sides of my intent, but only/ Vaulting ambition" (1.7.25-28). His strong ambition, not his rational mind pushes him to commit murder, and that is confirmed in Macbeth´s hallucinations before the regicide. At the night, when Macbeth decides do to an evil deed, he sees a dagger before his eyes, wondering if it was real: "A dagger of the mind, a false creation,/ Proceeding from the heat-oppressed brain " (2.1.38-39). The dagger begins to move towards Duncan´s room, and Macbeth is following it. So it seems that it is a dagger which forces Macbeth to commit the murder, but not his rational mind. As Johnston points out: "It is as if the dagger is pulling him toward the murder against his will - he is following an imagined projection of his desires, rather than being pushed into the murder by some inner passion" (1).

However, after the murder, Macbeth is tormented by his guilty consciousness and cannot live the same life with what he has done. Now Macbeth is thinking of his punishment as a lack of sleep, exclaiming: "Macbeth shall sleep no more" (2.2.40-2), and knowing that only innocent can normally sleep, he fears to sleep. In addition, his evil deed forces him to terrify himself, so that he assumes that his hands, which do not belong to him anymore, will distort his eyes: "What hands are these? Ha! They pluck out mine eyes" (2.2.58). Consequently, he regrets his crime and wishes to reverse the action, saying: Wake Duncan with thy knocking: I would thou couldst!" (2.2.73); but he knows that there is no further escape from the evil he chose.

Macbeth's crime obviously destroys the peace of his mind and soul, so he continues thinking that he must kill again in order to get the peace to his mind. In the third Act, again, Macbeth fears the justice he mentioned before the crime. Knowing about the prophecy for Banquo, who will acquire "the line of kings" (3.1.59),

Macbeth assumes that Banquo will kill him for the crown, and decides to murder him. He says: "There is none but he, whose being do I fear…, [and] for Banquo´s issue have I fill'd my mind; [for the same purpose] the gratious Duncan have I murther'd"(3.1.52, 64f). However, from this moment Macbeth has completely turned to the evil side because at now he never mentions his guilty consciousness, but only his fear to be killed. He does not hesitate any more in the immorality of the murder but continues murdering in order to get the piece to his mind. While Macbeth was struggling against his ambition in the first part of the play, now he absolutely subverts his good side to the evil.

Nevertheless, continuing to murder, Macbeth suffers from his evil deeds, because he continually loses the sense of human values which are so important in life. Bradley points out that "[t]he evil he has desperately embraced continues to madden or to wither his inmost heart" (365). Being social person at the beginning, Macbeth becomes alone at the end and isolates himself from the natural bond, which bears life and love in itself. According to Knight, "He is plunging deeper and deeper into unreality, the severance from mankind and all normal forms of life is now abysmal, deep" (155). This becomes obvious in his calm and uninterested reaction to his wife´s death: "She should have died hereafter. There should be time for such a word...Life [is] a walking world/ Signifying nothing" (5.5.16, 27). Macbeth does not care about his dead wife and his life anymore. He has obviously lost the sense of moral judgment, which will further lead to his own destruction. Macbeth, fallen in despair, realizes the consequences of his deed, that he following his own desires destroyed his previous life and himself. He reveals his despair several times: "I have liv´d long enough: my way of life/Is fall´n into the sear, the yellow leaf "(5.3.22-28), he further adds that "My soul is too much charg´d/ With blood" (5.8.5-6). Macbeth cannot bear the life he is living now, so that he decides to end this all in the final battle with Macduff, which should take place according to another witches´ prophecy (cf.4.1.90). When Macbeth goes into battle, he, as Blits points out, "...seems to be filled with a contradictory mixture of fear, confidence, and remorse" (192). There seems to be nothing left for him in his life that makes sense for him because Macbeth goes in the battle with assurance to resolve his suffering and dies heroically for his evil deeds.

So, there seems to be no doubt that Lear and Macbeth become the tragic heroes, who were the good characters at the beginning of the plays, but both of them became victims of evil. Lear becomes a tragic victim of the evil stemming from the evil deeds of his wicked daughters. Whereas Macbeth becomes a victim of his own evil, that is his own strong ambition leading him to a final destruction. So, it is obviously difficult to deal with human evil because evil leads to a destruction of goodness, as examples of Lear and Macbeth show. However, the medieval morality plays suggest that goodness should always win over evil because of man's repentance. So, the final chapter will be dealing with the problem of resolving evil and finding out if goodness can prevail over evilness in Shakespeare´s plays *King Lear* and *Macbeth*.

4. Resolving Evil? The Final Scenes

The interpretation of the final scenes in both plays gives an insight on what kind of force can actually prevail in the conflict of good and evil. In *King Lear*, Edgar, who was deceived by his villainous brother Edmund, and who by his words is a noble man, (cf.1.2.177) gets honoured with a royal throne. His goodness lies in his nobility, and the victory of his goodness over the villainy of Edmund, whom he defeated, compensates the tragic outcome of Lear´s and Cordelia´s fate. In his final words, Edgar regrets their death, saying: "[t]he weight of this sad time we must obey…" (5.3.322) and exits out of the final scene on music of a dead march, which reinforces the mood of grief. This sadness obviously signifies the great and unpredictable force of evil, which in the struggle with goodness, undesirably destroys it. However, despite of the tragic death of Lear and innocent Cordelia, Edgar's survival and his grate coronation imply the partial justice and victory of goodness in the struggle between good and evil.

The ending of *Macbeth* also leaves only one-sided triumph of goodness over evilness. Here Malcolm, the eldest son of Duncan, succeeds the throne on the basis of his birth (3.6.24-5). Malcolm, in contrast to his father, carefully addresses his thanes with the words: "So thanks to all at once and to each one" (5.9.40). In contrast to his father, who made friendship with Macbeth calling him the "worthiest cousin" (1.4.14), Malcolm avoids the potential danger of possible evil inflicted to his father without binding himself to any of his attendants. However, the final scene with crowning of Malcolm remains ambiguous one and its interpretations largely depends on the role of the witches at the end of the play. The witches, seen as the agents of devil in the seventeenth century controlling the man´s fate, do not perform such a role in *Macbeth*. Instead, they just appeal to the idea of what one wants to believe and do not have direct power to influence a man´s fate. For example, they do not tell Macbeth what he has to do in order to achieve the prophecy and they never appeal him to murder Duncan. Bradley points out that the witches are "symbolical representation of thoughts and desires" of Macbeth (316), he adds that they also represent "all those obscurer influences of the evil around him in the world which aid his own ambition" (348). So, the witches represent the potential evil desires of a man, and Macbeth´s destruction can be seen as a victory of goodness over evil. However, there is nothing said about the witches at the end of the play, so they are seemingly still present around near the new king Malcolm and his attendants. The evil of Macbeth is defeated, but the potential evil stemming from the witches´ appeals not. The play leaves an ambiguous victory of good over evil. Johnston compares the struggle of good and evil to a recurring cycle of light and darkness in which Malcolm´s light has permanently prevailed the forces of darkness. He concludes that "the play has not banished the darkness in the circle; it has simply brought back the circle of light" (1). In contrast to the morality plays, in which goodness is supposed to be always victorious in the struggle between good and evil, Shakespeare´s plays present the reader the ambiguous conflict of good and evil and do not give any certainty of a full victory for one force over the other.

The problem of the opposed forces lies not only in the ambiguity of the victory, but also in the clear classification of the characters to good and evil one. In comparison to morality plays in which the characters represent either virtues or vices, Shakespeare´s plays represent ambivalent characters, who cannot be seen as mere good (obviously except for Cordelia), or mere evil. Some fallibility is always presented in the good side of the character. For example, Banquo and Macbeth´s mental weakness eventually leads to their failure to resist enticement or Lear's pride leads him to be inferior to others. Moreover, there is also some virtue in the bad. For example, Edmund's repentance and Lady Macbeth's pity and compassion are virtues. The ambiguity of the characters can be compared to the Bacon's explanation of the colours of good and evil. He says that "[t]he forms [of good and evil] to make it conceived that that was evil which changed for the better... And of the other side, the forms to make it conceived that that was good which was changed for the worse..." (156). According to his statement the nature of good and evil is complex because of the changing feature of either colour. The characters, which also represent such a changing feature in their nature, appear to be morally complex, so that it is impossible to divide them clearly into good and evil. In addition, to call the characters evil is also unde- sirable because of their ambivalence. By that reason, they should be called bad characters rather than evil one. To be evil would mean to cause harm intentionally, and at the same time, it would mean to remain indifferent to the cruelty of one's own action. The charac- ters who are supposed to be evil such as Edmund, Lady Macbeth and Macbeth do not remain indifferent to what they have done, but rather they change their opinions or even suffer from what they have done. Such ambivalence also implies that the nature of man is as difficult as the nature of good and evil.

Moreover, the problem of the characters' complexity lies in man's nature and his freedom to choose actions. While in morality plays the source of good and evil is to be found in God and Devil, in Shakespeare's plays the source of wright and wrong comes from human actions. Hence, it is the question of ethics which deals with the problems of human's moral actions and man's nature which is as complex as his understanding of the moral values. The traditional moral values in the plays seem to represent the values of family bond, or to speak broadly, the values of life itself, these are also the values of the Renaissance age. In Shakespeare's plays, the characters do something ethically wrong because of their warped understanding of the moral values. So it seems that the inversion of the traditional moral values affects the character's actions, so that their vision of good appears to be in evil. In *King Lear,* Edmund and Lear act individually by denying the traditional family bonds. Machiavel Edmund sees his deception of his father and his brother as the source of his goodness and therefore, could get the throne. Lear sees the banishment of Cordelia as the source of his goodness because only so he can approve his royal prestige openly. In *Macbeth,* Macbeth and his wife see the plan of murdering Duncan as the source of their good because only so they can achieve the social prestige. This idea also implies that characters choosing morally wrong actions hope to achieve a good result. However, what the characters see as the source of their good is the actual source of evil because it undeniably leads to the evil consequences. The inversion of moral values leads to a destruction of other persons and finally to a self-destruction. In *King Lear*, Edmund´s source of good result in the tragic outcome of his father Gloucester, who suffers from knowing the truth of being deceived, and finally dies. Edmund is also defeated. Lear´s knowledge of the ingratitude of his daughters, and also his own error of judgment of Cordelia result in his suffering which goes to the point of madness. At the end of the play, he and the innocent Cordelia die. In *Macbeth*, Lady Macbeth and her husband´s source of good leads to the death of the innocent Duncan and Banquo, to their madness and to a lost lust on life and to death. So the characters´ source of good actually appears to be the source of evil, which leads to their destruction and finally to a self-destruction.

In addition, the problem of good and evil also leads to the confusion in understanding the true moral values in Shakespeare's plays. It seems to be difficult to conceive the moral values of Shakespeare on the first sight because what should be morally true, for example, Cordelia´s sincerity, fails. This also means what is morally good may have bad consequences. As Vyvyad puts it: "a surprising amount of confusion has been caused by failing to distinguish between Shakespeare´s values and those of his characters…" (12). However, it is possible to make some conclusions of what seems to be morally wrong in Shakespeare's plays. Shakespeare was living in the age, when the development and the new consciousness of individuals fostered the collapse of natural order of the medieval epoch. Shakespeare was seemingly against such destruction, so that he dramatizes the disruption of natural order in his plays. So, to be morally wrong in Shakespeare's plays would mean that every action of the characters causes the disruption of natural and moral order. In *Macbeth*, it is apparently the strong passion and the weaknesses of the characters' souls, who are unable to resist the temptation and follow their evil desires. In *King Lear,* it is the individual freedom expressed in the neglect of traditional order based on family and society bonds.

The problems that are dealt with in Shakespeare's *King Lear and Macbeth* still hold its relevance in today's society. Both tragedies reveal that the power of good and evil is multitudinous power because of its impact on people, especially that of the power of evil. Moreover, Shakespeare´s plays show that the power of evil is immense and cannot be easily resolved because of man´s temptation to use and to spread it. Bradley calls the power of evil "to be a poison", which is present in the world of Shakespeare's tragedies. He adds that "[t]he world [of the tragedy] reacts against [evil] violently, and, in the struggle to expel it, is driven to devastate itself" (304). That means evil causes harm for both who creates it and who struggles against it. This also suggests that the problems of good and evil cannot be possibly solved and humans will always imply the potential for creation of evil and destruction of goodness.

5. Conclusion

The first aim of this thesis was to identify to what extent the characters can be seen as good and evil. In the Renaissance, the moral qualities of good and evil behaviour were set according to the existing hierarchical order in the universe. Every person who tried to cause the disruption of natural and moral order was seen as an evil person. However, the late Renaissance was also regarded as a beginning of the modern era. During this period the hierarchical system of the universe was destroyed and the concepts of good and evil have changed. This thesis showed that the definition of good and evil has changed. In modern time, denial of traditional set of rules can be seen as an expression of one´s own individuality and do not mean to be evil, except for murder. Persons who commit murder were regarded and continue to be seen as evil persons. The characters in Shakespeare are not evil persons because the most of them do not commit murder, but behave morally wrong. So evil is too strong word for them, and they should be rather called wicked and bad persons. From all discussed characters, Macbeth is the most evil person because he murders, but again he suffers from his own evil deeds. Although Macbeth acted beyond accepted wrongdoing, he was in an ambitious state and acted from emotional grounds, so he is not an evil person by his nature.

The second aim of this thesis was to explore the problems of the concepts of good and evil in terms of the tragedies. The problems of good and evil are many sided and cannot be easily solved because of its ambiguous nature. The first problem refers to the characters´ classification to good and bad. To define the characters as good and bad is problematic because of their ambivalent depiction (except for Cordelia, who does not change her good nature throughout the play). The discussed characters are depicted ambiguous because of their free will and freedom of choice between good and evil. For example, Banquo reveals transition from good to bad because of his ambiguous goodness. On the one hand, he has guilty consciousness to keep secret from Duncan; on the other hand, he hopes to get power on the cats of Macbeth´s crime. Moreover, Edmund and Lady Macbeth show change from bad to good. Edmund deceives his father and brother but repents before his death because he feels compassion to his dead father. Lady Macbeth wishing to kill Duncan becomes mad after the murder made by Macbeth. Her madness reveals her true woman nature. In addition, Lear shows transition from good to bad, while Macbeth changes from good to evil because he acts beyond "normal" wrongdoing. Lear reveals a good personality of being a king. However, he is not so good because of his pride and individual traits. Finally, he regrets his deeds and becomes good again in revealing his love to Cordelia. Macbeth is a good warrior who changes to evil because he murders because of his inability to self-restrain.

Moreover, the thesis revealed that the problem of good and evil also lies in understanding of moral values, which differ from person to person. In modern time, it is the question of ethics which defines the norms of behaviour as moral and immoral. Depending on the circumstances, moral values differ from character to character in both plays. While Cordelia accepts traditional values of a family, Edmund and Lear act individually by denying these traditional values. Lady Macbeth and Macbeth acknowledge murder to be morally wrong but they are unable to control their self-restrain and act on emotional grounds. However, what all characters see as a source of their good becomes actually the source of their evil because their wrongdoings lead to the evil consequences, namely to the destruction of others and their own destruction. From these results it follows what actually is morally bad in Shakespeare. Shakespeare dramatizes every action which is beyond the norms of Renaissance traditional views of natural and moral order. In terms of the plays it is denial of family bonding and wish to follow own evil desires which can harm other people. It again confirms the fact that moral values have been changed from Renaissance to modern era. Moreover, Shakespeare´s plays reveal that moral goodness can have bad consequences, whereas immorality may have a good result. For example, Cordelia´s sincerity was rejected by Lear while Machiavellian tactics helped Edmund to get the power.

In addition, the thesis showed that the problem of the concepts also lies in the ambiguous victory of one force over the other. Both plays reveal only the partial victory of good over evil, what implies that evil potentially exists in human. It is expressed in the witches, who still present at the end in *Macbeth* and who represent the potential evil desires of a man. In addition, the power of evil is immense, because innocent and naive goodness can be easily destructed by human evil, as an example of innocent Cordelia showed, and creator of evil can be punished as well.

Bibliography

Primary Literature

Bacon, Francis (1900) *The Essays: Colours of Good and Evil & Advancement of Learning.* New York: Macmillan.

Machiavelli, Niccolo (2004) *The Prince.* London: Penguin.

Montaigne, Michel Eyquem de (1958) *The Complete Essays of Montaigne.* Trans. Donald Frame. Stanford: Stanford UP.

Shakespeare, William (1997) *King Lear.* Ed. R.A. Foakes. London: The Arden Shakespeare.

Shakespeare, William (1984) *Macbeth.* Ed. Kenneth Muir. London: The Arden Shakespeare.

Secondary Literature

Anderson, David K. (2011) "The Tragedy of Good Friday: Sacrificial Violence in *King Lear.*" *Violence in Literature* 78.2: 259-286.

Beauregard, David N. (2008) "Human Malevolence and Providence in *King Lear.*" *Renascence* 60.3: 199-271.

Blits, Jan H. (1996) *The Insufficiency of Virtue:* Macbeth *and the Natural Order.* Lanham: Rowman, Littlefield.

Bradley, A.C. (1967) *Shakespearean Tragedy: Lectures on* Hamlet, Othello, King Lear, Macbeth. New York: Macmillan.

Bradley, Lynne (2010) *Adapting* King Lear *for the Stage.* Burlington: Ashgate.

Burckhardt, Jacob (1955) *The Civilization of the Renaissance in Italy.* Trans. S.G. Middlemore. New York: Phaidon.

Coe, Charles N. (1972) *Shakespeare's Villains.* New York: AMS Press.

Formosa, Paul (2007) "Understanding Evil Acts." *Human Studies* 30.2: 57-77.
Hazlitt, William (1949) *Characters of Shakespeare's Plays.* London: Oxford UP.
Johnston, Jan (1999) "Introduction to *Macbeth.*" *Studies in Shakespeare.* 1 Dec. 2011
http://records.viu.ca/~johnstoi/eng366/lectures/macbeth.htm

Johnston, Jan (1999) " Speak What We Feel: An Introduction to *King Lear.*" *Studies in Shakespeare.* 1 Dec. 2011
http://records.viu.ca/~johnstoi/eng366/lectures/lear.htm

The Oxford English Dictionary. Oxford: Oxford UP.

Kirsch, Arthur (1990) *The Passions of Shakespeare's Tragic Heroes*. Charlottesville: Virginia UP.

Kirschbaum, Leo (1945) "Shakespeare's 'Good' and 'Bad'." *The Review of English Studies* 21.82: 136-142.

Knight, Wilson G. (1961) *The Wheel of Fire: Interpretations of Shakespearean Tragedy*. London: Methuen.

Lökse, Olav (1960) *Outrageous Fortune: Critical Studies in* Hamlet *and* King Lear. Oslo: Oslo UP.

Roe, John (2002) *Shakespeare and Machiavelli*. Cambridge: Cambridge UP.

Ryan, Kiernan (2005) King Lear: *William Shakespeare*. New York: Macmillan.

Spencer, Theodore (1961) *Shakespeare and the Nature of Man*. New York: Macmillan.

Spivack, Charlotte (1978) *The Comedy of Evil on Shakespeare's Stage*. Rutherford: Fairleigh Dickinson UP.

Tung, Alexander C. (2011) *The Visionary Shakespeare*. Taipei: Showwe Information.

Tufts, Carol S. (1998) " Shakespeare´s Conception of Moral Order in *Macbeth*." *Renascence* 50.3: 169-183.

Vyvyad, John (1959) *The Shakespearean Ethic*. London: Chatto, Windus.

White, R.S. (1986) *Innocent Victims: Poetic Injustice in Shakespearean Tragedy*. 2[nd]ed. London: Athlone.